LAUGH OUT LOUD

FUNNY POEMS CHOSEN BY
FIONA WATERS
Illustrated by Jane Eccles

MACMILLAN CHILDREN'S BOOKS

First published 2008 by Macmillan Children's Books
a division of Macmillan Publishers Limited
20 New Wharf Road, London N1 9RR
Basingstoke and Oxford
Associated companies throughout the world
www.panmacmillan.com

ISBN 978-0-330-45456-8

1 3 5 7 9 8 6 4 2

A CIP catalogue record for this book is available from
the British Library.

Typeset by Nigel Hazle
Printed and bound in the UK by CPI Mackays, Chatham ME5 8TD

Laugh Out Loud

Fiona Waters is one of the most prolific and very best anthologists in the children's book world. Her work includes *Love, Don't Panic: 100 Poems to Save Your Life*, *Wizard Poems*, *Best Friends* and *Christmas Poems*. Her unparalleled knowledge of poetry and children's books has come about, in part, through Fiona's previous incarnations as a book-seller, publisher, reviewer, author and her current position as Editorial Director of Troubadour, the highly successful school-book-fair company.

Fiona lives in Dorset, surrounded by thousands of books and some very discerning cats.

Jane Eccles has been laughing out loud for many years now. She often laughs out loud when watching a funny film or reading a funny book. She certainly laughed out loud an awful lot when illustrating the poems in this book, and hopes you do too.

She lives in Hampshire with her husband and son, who are also known to laugh out loud on occasion.

For Spike, with love from
your favourite eccentric
GAF

Contents

The Laughter Forecast

Today will be humorous
With some giggly patches,
Scattered outbreaks of chuckling in the south
And smiles spreading from the east later,
Widespread chortling
Increasing to gale-force guffaws towards evening.
The outlook for tomorrow
Is hysterical.

Sue Cowling

Days

It's funny how Mister Tomorrow
can turn into Mrs Today.
They write to each other quite often
inviting each other to stay,

But Mister Tomorrow is dreamy.
He always forgets what is said
until it's too late for a meeting
and Mrs Today is in bed.

It's funny how Mister Tomorrow
is partial to picnics and treats.
He'll call for a basket to borrow
and fill it with jellies and sweets –

But Mrs Today is too busy.
With a hanky to hold back her hair
she's clearing up yesterday's muddle
and hasn't a moment to spare.

Jean Kenward

My Granny Is in Love with That Weird Weather Forecaster on the Six o'Clock News

She dreams
    that he sweeps
        her away
            in her slippers

They dance
    through the night
        then she cooks
            him some kippers

Lindsay Macrae

Some Day, My Prince

Kiss . . . . . . Croak
Kiss . . . . . . Croak
Kiss . . . . . . Croak
Kiss . . . . . . Croak

I'll find that flipping prince
if I have to kiss
every frog in this pond.

Mike Jubb

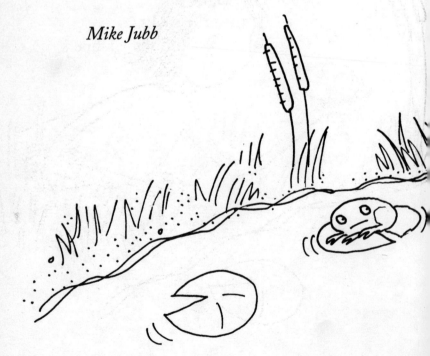

Bigger and Better

I'm going to do something bigger and better,
bigger and better
and bolder, but first
I'm going to do something
smaller and worse.

Jon Arno Lawson

Who's a Lovely Girl?

Well, who's a lovely girl then?
(Not me, you stupid bat.)
And who's got shiny hair then?
(You'd think I was the cat.)

You're so much like your mummy.
(I think I'm just like me.)
With little bits of Grandma.
(I have to disagree.)

And, wow, you have grown taller!
(That's what we humans do.)
And who's a clever girl then?
(Obviously not you.)

Steve Turner

Goggles

I lost my green goggles
in the grey, misty foggles
when walking my doggles

I looked under loggles
and asked the hedgehoggles
if they'd seen my goggles

then I found my green goggles
y'know the mind really boggles
– they were on two little froggles

John Rice

When I Was a Pirate

And when I was a pirate
One of my legs was wooden,
Since then it's grown back again
Though doctors said it couldn't.

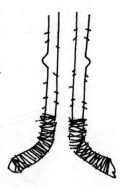

And when I was a pirate
I'd a parrot that could talk,
But now I'm dad to seven kids
Who only screech and squawk.

And when I was a pirate
I sailed the Seven Seas,
But now I wait at bus stops
And shop at Sainsbury's.

And when I was a pirate
I wore a black eyepatch,
But now I need my glasses on
To watch a football match.

And when I was a pirate
I was scary with a sword.
Now, though I go: 'Excuse me, please!'
I usually get ignored.

And when I was a pirate
I owned a treasure chest,
But now I earn a weekly wage
And bank it with NatWest.

And when I was a pirate
My coat was spun from gold,
But now I wear an anorak
With the hood up when it's cold.

11

And when I was a pirate
I was hairy, with a beard,
But now my head is shiny
And my hair has disappeared.

And when I was a pirate
I'd five fingers and a hook,
But the day that we were married
That's the first thing my wife took.
She said, 'Get real! You'll need both hands
To wash and clean and cook!'

And when I was a pirate
I was merciless and cruel . . .
And I still am, because I make
My children go to school!

Nick Toczek

Persevering Percival

I am Persevering Percival,
relentless in my quest,
my thirst is quite unquenchable,
I never let things rest.
I'm gritty and I'm merciless,
I'm firm and resolute,
I persist when others weaken,
and stay fixed in my pursuit.

I'm unshakeable, unbreakable,
you cannot make me bend,
I am Persevering Percival –
I do what I intend.
I am stubborn, staunch and steadfast,
for I have a one-track mind,
and to what does not concern me
I am absolutely blind.

I am totally unyielding,
as tenacious as can be,
there is no one so decisive
and unwavering as me.
Yes, I'm Persevering Percival,
resolved to see things through . . .
if I only could determine
what it is I'm going to do.

Graham Denton

The Great Dog's Dinner Robbery

Alfie is the toughest of the gangster cats
Black and white suit, green eyes, white spats
He swaggers up and down our little house
Ignores the budgie, forgets the mouse.

He's heard a free meal is in the offing
Knows what Bozo the dog is scoffing
Whipping his paw in the dog's fat face
Alfie jumps in the bowl, invades his space.

He twitches his tail, waves it, flicks it
Begins to eat poor Bozo's biscuit
Eats all the best bits of Bozo's meat
Then slips away on his soft-soled feet.

Bozo is gobsmacked, Bozo is shocked
His ears go up, head half-cocked
He sniffs at his bowl, it's empty and bare
Everything's gone, it's just not there!

He barks and snuffles, starts to whine
Wasn't that dinner supposed to be mine?
But it's disappeared, that is that
Bozo's dinner is inside the cat.

Alfie stretches, licking his paw
A real cool cat, no fear of The Law
He sidles off softly to meet The Mob
Laugh at poor Bozo and plan the next job.

David Harmer

Night Sky in the Clun Valley

(for Vincent)

The sky is throwing out woks,
The moon is munching bananas,
The stars wear sparkly socks,
The planets are harbouring llamas.

Chrissie Gittins

Eco-logic

If motor cars were changed to green,
We'd have an eco-sensation.
If motor cars were changed to pink,
We'd have a pink car-nation.

Ian Larmont

Abominable Poem

Tick-tock . . . tick-tock . . . tick-tock . . .
Mooooooooooooooo
BOOM!
That's a bomb in a bull.

Nick Toczek

The Reason for the Pelican

The reason for the pelican
Is difficult to see:
His beak is clearly larger
Than there's any need to be.

It's not to bail a boat with –
He doesn't own a boat.
Yet everywhere he takes himself
He has that beak to tote.

It's not to keep his wife in –
His wife has got one too.
It's not a scoop for eating soup.
It's not an extra shoe.

It isn't quite for anything.
And yet you realize
It's really quite a splendid beak
In quite a splendid size.

John Ciardi

Escape Plan

As I, Stegosaurus
stand motionless
in the museum
I am secretly planning
my escape

At noon
Tyrannosaurus rex
will cause a diversion
by wheeling around the museum's high ceilings
and diving at the curators and museum staff
while I
quietly slip out of the fire exit
and melt
into the London crowds

Roger Stevens

Bird Brain

An ostrich from Ipswich was itching and
  scratching
and stretching his neck for a flea needed catching.

He swivelled around so his head and beak pointed
right back where he'd come from, contorted,
  disjointed,

then poised and prepared to attack, but the flea
leaped out from his feathers, acrobatically,

and looped through the air like a stunt aeroplane.
The ostrich looped too, without using his brain –

his neck got twisted and tied in a knot
so tightly that from that day ostrich forgot

just everything! From the neck up he was blank,
not even remembering – a flea was to thank.

Gina Douthwaite

The Creepicle's Tail

A creepicle crept
when the cook was asleep
to scrobbage the kitchen
for scraps.
By a josset of ogg
stood a chumbly cake,
and a jiffle
with flamberry snaps.

He took just a snickle,
a nobbler of ogg,
just a nizzle of
flamberry snap,
then he danced on the jiffle
with muffeted paws
and his bobbery tail
slipper-slap.

The slippety-slap
woke the cook, who screethed
at the sight of the flummertiquake.
'Who has danced on my jiffle
and clarted the cream?
Who has snickled
my chumbly cake?'

But the creepicle dimsied
home to his hole
to dream of
the yumsicle snack,
with his muffeted paws
on his bellibous tum
and his bobbery tail
at the back.

Irene Rawnsley

Laughing Your Head Off

When your belly shakes
and your shoulders jiggle
when you know what's coming
is bigger than a giggle.

When you gasp for breath
and your face turns blue
when your legs turn to jelly
and you really need the loo.

When your jaw is aching
and your nose starts to drip
when you make a noise
like a foghorn on a ship.

When you're snorting like a pig
and you're clucking like a hen
when you thought you'd finished
but you only start again.

When your eyes turn to water
and you start to cry
when you're roaring like a lion
and you don't know why.

When you're blaring like a trumpet
and you splutter and you cough
that's what you do
when you're laughing your head off.

Craig Bradley

Two Giraffes in a Mini

There were two giraffes in a Mini car
(one of them was learning)
but they were so uncomfortable
they stopped at the Necks Turning.

Jill Townsend

Hair Growing

Hair grows a centimetre a month
Or a third of a millimetre a day.
That means
That while you've been reading this poem
Your hair
(And mine)
Will have grown
A billimetre,
A trillimetre,
A zillimetre
Or a squillimetre!
It depends how fast you read.

Sue Cowling

Beauty Sleeping

The young prince was handsome,
    Dashing and bold,
His armour was silver,
    His hair gleamed like gold.
He galloped about –
    As a handsome prince should –
Berating the baddies,
    Assisting the good.

Then he came to a garden
    So thorny and thick
He could hardly get in there.
    He found a big stick,
Beat his way to the door
    Then forced his way through.
The stairs rose before him
    And up them he flew.

He discovered a chamber,
    A dull, dusty room,
Where an army of spiders
    Wove webs in the gloom.
A beautiful princess
    Lay sleeping inside.
He unbuckled his armour
    And rushed to her side.

He bent down his head
    And gave her a kiss ...
But she rose from her pillow
    And said, with a hiss ...
'What are you doing?
    Get off me, you creep!
How dare you awake me
    From my beauty sleep!'

Jennifer Curry

Limerick

There once was a widow from Parma
Who wooed a Peruvian farmer.
He hadn't a horse
And so in due course
They eloped on the back of a llama.

Sue Cowling

Teacher's Report

English literature – weak: this term
he has probably not read anything more gruesome
than Peter Rabbit, cabbage chewer

English language – sad: lacks understanding
of everyday speech – thinks cool is
the temperature of school soup

Maths – illogical: when he sees
a boy, a ruler and a small lump of chewed paper,
he does not put two and two together

Current affairs – poor: he displays
shocking ignorance of *Big Brother*, soap-star
    scandals
and Saturday-morning TV programmes

Science – mad: reacts easily, spouts gas, fizzes,
turns bright red, then blows his top

History – good: but then he ought to be –
he's lived through it all

Dave Calder

A Lesson

Darren took all
the labels off
the tins in Mummy's
shopping bag.

He sorted them
like teacher had,
red and yellow,
green and blue.

Tonight the dog
had soup for tea,
the cat had beans
and Darren had

Whiskas.
He said it
tasted horrible
on toast.

Brian Morse

Hot Dog

'We're having a puppy for Christmas!'
My friend said, bright and perky;
And I replied, 'Oh, gosh – that's sad!
We always have a turkey ...!'

Trevor Harvey

Baby Change

I tried to change my brother
for one that didn't yell,
wake me every morning
or make an awful smell.
But they didn't have another,
there were not any there –
just a plastic table
and a little baby chair.
I tried to swap my brother
for one that didn't cry
but the changing place
was empty
and there wasn't one to buy.

Peter Dixon

← Baby
Changing

On the Twelfth Day of Christmas

On the twelfth day of Christmas
my friend said 'Come and see –'
twelve bags of rubbish
eleven empty bottles

ten tatty streamers
nine broken baubles
eight crumpled crackers
seven chocolate wrappers
six sad satsumas

five soggy sprouts –
four late Christmas cards

three crushed cans
two dead batteries
and a beard underneath the settee!

Sue Cowling

The Stinker Stunk

Somebody let off a stink bomb one day
Next to me, at the back of the class.
  We thought that the teacher would holler and
      shout –
  We never considered she might stick it out,
So the whole thing turned into a farce!

She carried on reading aloud! Not a sign
That her nostrils were being attacked!
  And we got the worst of it, being so near!
  Our lungs were assaulted, and many a tear
Filled our eyes, and our voices were cracked.

The smell was disgusting! Like really bad eggs,
And it hovered around where we sat,
  Cos someone had closed all the windows before
  To keep the stink in – oh, it made our throats
      sore!
And the teacher read on – the old bat!

The smell seemed to change as it drifted around:
It was just like my brother's old socks,
   Or perhaps a ripe kipper found under the bed,
   The stink of an ashtray, or someone who's dead,
Or the sharp, pungent smell of a fox.

And still she kept reading! Our joke had misfired
And we silently prayed for the bell,
   For the smell was like sewers, or flower-water
      dregs,
   Or Brussels sprouts cooking, or stinking bad
      eggs –
Could no one release us from hell?

Pam Gidney

Photo Opportunity

I'm waiting in line
For the class photo
I'm getting my face ready
Trying out
A few expressions
A few good looks:

casual
hard
INTERESTING
cool

I think I'll go
For **casual**-*cool*
And wait for the shutter to click.
Clunk!

So
How come
When the photos come back
In their 'special offer' pack
I look just like I did
(Just another soppy kid)
Last time?

Trevor Millum

Not Today, Missus

Miss Crumb, on the beach, found a bottle.
Funny shape, coloured blue, rather weird.
And then from the spout
misty vapour poured out,
and a whacking great genie appeared.

Miss Crumb cried aloud: 'How ecstatic!
He'll grant me some wishes for sure.
A prince I'll request,
quite exquisitely dressed,
with a palace and riches galore.'

She made her wish known to the genie,
who replied with a cough and a croak:
'You're out of luck, missus.
No time for your wishes.
I've only popped out for a smoke.'

Barry Buckingham

Limericks

The elephant never forgets,
He always repays all his debts;
   So if you treat him ill,
   His trunk he will fill
And soak you with huge jumbo jets.

A shark makes a marvellous pet.
It is cuddly if rather wet.
   It won't make much noise,
   And it *loves* girls and boys,
And will really astonish the vet!

Gerard Benson

The Owl and the Pussycat

The owl and the pussycat
Went to sea
The owl ate the pussycat
Oh deary me

Roger Stevens

Big Fat Budgie

I'm a big fat budgie,
I don't do a lot.
Might park on my perch.
Might peck in my pot.
Might peek at my mirror.
Might ring my bell.
Might peer through the bars of my fat budgie cell.
Might say, 'Who's a pretty boy then?'
Might not.
I'm a big fat budgie.
I don't do a lot.

Michaela Morgan

With a Dad Like This, Who Needs Enemies?

A dad with shorts
As baggy and wrinkled as an elephant's skin
Parading his pink and hairy knees all summer
Who does Tom Jones impressions
In the middle of a crowded street
Just as I walk past him with my friends.

A dad who all of a sudden
Very loudly walks and talks like a mad robot
In the checkout queue at the supermarket
And who makes mysterious whoopee-cushion
    noises
Every time he runs upstairs.

A dad who jokes about the clothes I wear
And who hates my music, who argues
With my teacher, the woman at the garage
Shop assistants and the boy at the burger bar
Because French fries aren't proper chips.

A dad who pulls faces at me
When I'm on the school bus and who talks
In silly voices to all my friends, the kind of dad
Everyone else thinks is great
But nobody else has to live with him
They don't know how tough that is!

David Harmer

One thing not to think about stuck in a traffic jam on the M5

A bag of chips
vinegary lips
a bag of chips.

Another thing not to think about stuck in a traffic jam on the M5

The loo.

Judith Green

Haiku

My surfacing toes
reflected in bath water:
two Cornish pasties!

Celia Warren

I Took My Dog to a Movie

I took my dog to a movie –
My dog was gripped throughout;
He didn't shuffle in his seat,
He didn't kick about.

He fixed upon the picture
And he followed every scene –
Not once was he distracted
From the action on the screen.

He sat there captivated
As he watched the plot unfold,
From the moment that it opened
Till the closing credits rolled.

Yes, I took my dog to a movie
And a chord it must have struck.
It's really most peculiar –
He didn't like the book!

Graham Denton

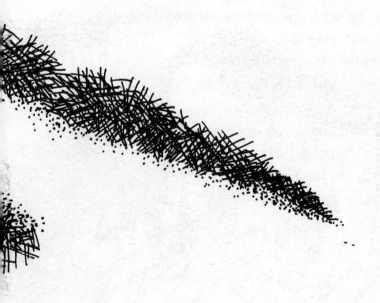

Identity Fraud

My copycat, he copies cats
in everything they do.
One moment he's a ginger tom,
the next a Persian blue.

And if he sees a Siamese
he'll follow it around
whilst mimicking its almond eyes
and squealing, chatty sound.

For life with this impressionist
is never, ever dull –
last night he was a kitten
playing with a ball of wool.

He watched a lion once on TV,
then changed from head to toe.
With golden mane he left
to stalk a water buffalo.

Why, he can be a tail-less Manx,
or any other mog.
He writes down every cat he's been
in his huge catalogue.

No imitation is too hard,
he's never in a flap.
It's wonderful to have
a Bengal tiger on your lap.

My copycat, he copies cats
in everything they do.
If you're a cat now reading this,
watch out! – he'll copy you.

Stewart Henderson

Nothing Doing

Mr Newton blew a gasket –
    he just flew into a rage,
when the homework that I passed him
    had no words upon the page.

'If I had a million dollars . . .'
    Mr Newton had us write,
which is why I handed over
    just the blankest sheet of white.

'You've done nothing!' the teacher hollered.
    'Yes,' I told him, 'that is true –
if I had a million dollars
    that's *precisely* what I'd do!'

Graham Denton

Auntie's Boyfriend

(for Brian and Lu, with love)

Auntie's brought her boyfriend home. He's sitting
   in a chair.
   He wears an earring and he's got no hair.

He's crazy about football and I'm glad about that.
He's polite to Granny, he's kind to the cat,
But I have to make an effort not to stand and
   stare
   Cos he wears an earring and he's got no hair.

He eats his dinner nicely. His manners are OK.
He sips his tea in silence in an ordinary way.
He nibbles with decorum at a chocolate eclair –
   But he wears an earring and he's got no hair.

I'll ring up the gang. I'll ring them for a dare:
'Come round this evening, there's a secret I must
   share.
Auntie's brought her boyfriend home. He's sitting
   in a chair
And he wears an earring and he's got no hair.'

Fred Sedgwick

Grandma Was Eaten by a Shark

Grandma was eaten by a shark
Dad by a killer whale
And my baby brother got slurped up
By a rather hungry sea snail

A cuttlefish cut my mum to bits
An octopus strangled my sister
A jellyfish stung my auntie's toes
Giving her terrible blisters

A pufferfish poisoned my grandpa
A dogfish ate my cat
And then a catfish ate my dog!
I was very upset about that

So you go for a swim if you like
Just don't ask me to come too
I'm staying here with my camera
I can't wait to see what gets you!

Andrea Shavick

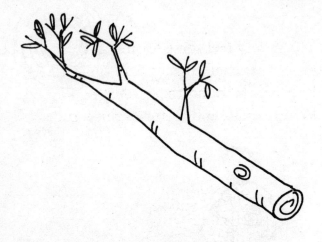

Funny Punny Haiku

I was chopping trees
when the Queen was passing by.
I gave her a bough.

Jill Townsend

Slug

You should feel sorry for the slug –
He has no shell to keep him snug
But slithers round the garden, nude,
Which snails and tortoises think rude.

Hedgehogs, however, think they're swell:
Easy to eat without a shell.

Pam Gidney

What Scientists Have Concluded from the Fact That So Many *Plant*-eating Dinosaurs Were of the Extra-large, Oversize, Super, Bumper, Jumbo, Giant, Mega, Massive, Vast Variety . . .

Eating shrubbery
leaves you blubbery.

Graham Denton

Going to Gran's

I like to visit my gran
it's always lots of fun
but she's ever so keen
on keeping things clean
so there's lots of jobs to be done

we beat out the mat
where the cats have sat
and hoover dog hairs
off the stairs;
but that's just the start
because gran likes things smart

we have to
brush the dust off the platypus
tidy bored toads into the wardrobe
push the rhino off the lino
dig the gopher out of the sofa
put the llamas in their pyjamas
tuck an armadillo under each pillow
pull parakeets out of the sheets
and give the giraffe a bath

you'd think that was enough
but gran's an awful fuss:
she makes
me shake the snakes
and iron the lion
before we get tea and cakes.

Dave Calder

75

Home Sweet Home

Mrs Magpie (loud and grumpy)
Squawked, 'This nest is far too lumpy.
Far too breezy round my legs.
Far too scruffy for my eggs.'

Mr Magpie flapped his wings,
Swooped and searched for shiny things,
Gifts to please his noisy bride –
Brought them back with speed and pride.

Mrs Magpie squawked again . . .
'Where's your sense and where's your brain?
Shiny things won't mend the floor.
Swap this useless junk for straw.'

Mr Magpie (slightly stressed)
Fluttered east and fluttered west
Till he spied an ancient mat,
Frayed by feet and clawed by cat.

Mrs Magpie squawked with joy ...
'Doormat strands! You clever boy!'
All that week, the busy birds
Fixed their nest with woven words.

Now the happy magpies greet
Feathered friends with, 'Wipe your feet!'
And when their chicks have fledged and flown,
Their nest will still say 'WELCOME HOME'.

Clare Bevan

Tell Me Another One

A tall-tale teller
And a tell-tale teller
Told tales together.
The tall-tale teller
Said his were true.
'Oooo,' said the tell-tale teller,
'I'll tell on you.'
And he did.

Catherine Benson

The Snake

The kiss of a snake
arrives at the tip
of a double-pronged tongue.

So make no mistake:
If a kiss has two tips
instead of two lips

you'd better run.

Jon Arno Lawson

Sharks Don't Bark

Sharks don't bark
or sniff or cough or sneeze,
sharks don't bark
when they're heading for your knees.

Sharks don't bark
and they have a radar nose,
the Great White thinks you're edible,
especially your toes.

Sharks don't bark
or yell or growl or yelp
and some are rather playful.
Watch them rolling through the kelp.

They can hear and sense and smell you
even though you're not in view;
they're solitary and sociable,
and curious like you.

Sharks don't bark
and even if they could,
would they still be tabloid outcasts,
maligned, misunderstood?

Sharks don't bark –
you're not their chosen meal,
it's really not their fault
they mistook you for a seal.

Stewart Henderson

A Fever

I've got A fever
So, aardvarks, aeroplanes, apes and antelopes
Aerosols, anteaters, aspirins and Action Men
Acorns, alligators, aliens and astronauts
Asteroids, acrobats, angles and amplifiers
All make me itch and sneeze and cough.

My brother Zak's got Z fever
Can't go to the zoo, or subtract zero
Can't cross on a zebra, sneezes at zigzags
Zips and zeitgeists, zeniths and zodiacs
Can't even say his own name.

My auntie Julie's got Y fever
Hates Yorkies, yogurt, yachts and yule logs
Yokes and yawning, yeast and yellowhammers
Comes out in a rash when somebody says
'I saw you yesterday, you know.'

Uncle Jack has B fever
Sister Dawn has E fever
Cousin Masefield has C fever
But me, I've got A fever.

So, artichokes, A levels, albums and antibodies
Alloys, aviaries, allspice and armpits
Admin, admen, admirals and allegories
All make me itch, cough and sneeze
Can't even watch *Andy Pandy* or *The A-Team*
Cos me, I've got A fever.
Achoooo!

David Harmer

A selected list of titles available from Macmillan Children's Books

The prices shown below are correct at the time of going to press. However, Macmillan Publishers reserves the right to show new retail prices on covers, which may differ from those previously advertised.

I'd Rather Be a Footballer Chosen by Paul Cookson	**978-0-330-45713-2**	**£4.99**
Read Me – **10th Anniversary Edition** Chosen by Gaby Morgan	**978-0-330-45716-3**	**£6.99**
Jingle Bells – **Poems for Christmas** Chosen by Gaby Morgan	**978-0-330-45715-6**	**£4.99**

All Pan Macmillan titles can be ordered from our website, www.panmacmillan.com, or from your local bookshop and are also available by post from:

Bookpost, PO Box 29, Douglas, Isle of Man IM99 1BQ
Credit cards accepted. For details:
Telephone: 01624 677237
Fax: 01624 670923
Email: bookshop@enterprise.net
www.bookpost.co.uk

Free postage and packing in the United Kingdom